Lab Fever

For information on other Willow Creek Press titles, call 1-800-850-9453

Printed in the United States

Lab Fever

Living, Loving and Laughing with America's #1 Pet

by Bruce Cochran

Willow Creek
P R E S S

MINOCQUA, WISCONSIN

"Why can't you just hang out the window like other dogs?"

"When I said 'sit' that wasn't exactly what I had in mind!"

"They do have a tendency to become part of the family, don't they?"

"I'm going for a W-AL-K without the D-O-G."

"Oh no! My wife and my best friend!"

"He likes you."

"No no. Just OUR newspaper."

"You forgot to give him a dog biscuit."

COCHRAN!

"Yes, I own a black lab. Why do you ask?"

"Yes, I own a Labrador retriever. Why do you ask?"

"Do you really have to go out or is this just another con job?"

"She heard you say we were all going for ice cream."

"He wants you to take him swimming."

"Do you realize our dog comes from a better family than we do?"

"Forsaking all others means HUMAN others."

"At first, he just wanted me to THROW the tennis ball . . ."

COCHRAN!

"No no! Not HERE! Wait till you're closer to THEM!"

"He's always like this the night before a big field trial."

"Be nice to her, she's thirty-five. That's 245 in dog years."

"I know you like to play with socks, but can't you wait till I take it off?"

"That's how they get acquainted."

"Why can't you just lie on the couch like other dogs?"

"He beat out four high school kids for the job."

"Is it thundering again?"

COCHRAN!

"How can you face down a ten-pound honker but be afraid of a cat?"

"And we wondered how he would react to the sweeper . . . "

"He wants you to pet him."

"How many Lassie videos did you rent for him this time?"

" . . . but the third little pup was bought by yuppies who made him wear a bandana around his neck and do tricks."

"Postman's here."

"Do you have a seat where he can hang out the window?"

"Usually he just pees on them."

"How many times have I told you not to beg?"

"No, Mrs. Jenkins. The dog didn't eat my homework. But he retrieved it so many times it was all slimey."

COCHRAN!

"How does he lie down without turning around three times first?"

"How the hell can you turn twenty pounds of dog food into 120 pounds of poop?!"

"Look, Bruno. A new chewy toy."

"Where's Jake? I sent him to fetch me a beer thirty minutes ago."

"Who needs to work out? I get enough exercise stepping over the dog all day."

"Now wait till he sits down, then go to the door like you want out."

COCHRAN!

"Of course it's hot in here! She's laying on the air conditioning vent!"

"How many times have I told you not to jump up on people?"

"She never sleeps well in a motel room."

"Okay. What else besides a poodle bitch in heat wearing nothing but a rhinestone collar?"

"We'll take it."

"How do you expect me to see a red light when my windshield is all slobbered up?"

"At first we didn't care when you brought your dog to the office, Winslow. However . . ."

"Sure, he hunts. He hunts for a place to lie down, he hunts for something to eat . . ."

"I'm bored. Let's walk through the living room and see how many things we can knock off the tables with our tails."

"Looks like Lady's in heat again."

"She wants to go for a ride."

"Well well. Man's best friend. And a dog, too."

"She fetched it. Let her read it."

"Now you know how I feel when you lie in my chair."

"Your order is here . . ."

"She's not biting you. She just wants to carry you around in her mouth for a while."

"He always goes straight to the one person in the room who doesn't like dogs."

"He's not so smart. He can't program the VCR either."

"I want this vanilla one!"

"It's an electronic collar. I have to be good while I'm wearing it."

"If you don't mind, we'd like a little privacy."

"Dinner time already?"

"You can have the house, the car, the boat. Just leave me Buster!"

COCHRAN!

"He must be eight or nine years old. He's getting gray around the muzzle."

"Don't worry. I won't go without you."

"Shot time again?"

"Does the term 'no' ring a bell with you?"

"He doesn't bite, but he might lick you to death."

"Who'll volunteer to give Bruno his pill? How about you, Tammy? You've still got all your fingers."

COCHRON!

"No need to wash this plate, Mom. Buster's licked it clean."

"I TOLD you labs were great with kids."

"Come on back to my place, baby. And I'll show you my field trial trophies."

COCHRAN!

"At least he doesn't chew the furniture anymore."

"Sure. I was the pick of the litter. But it was a very small litter."

"He used to bark at the postman. Now he barks when I have e-mail."

"How come you can hear the can opener but not the whistle?"

"Is it my imagination or is Jake shedding more this summer?"

"He's taking me to the park."

"Eager to please, isn't he?"

COCHRAN!

"Get your head in, Bucky, before the guy behind us has to turn on his wipers."

"I see we need a little more work on the 'heel' command!"

"He hates frisbees."

"They do love water, don't they?"